Ages 3+

## Trace with Me

# Tracing Numbers

3

3 3 3 3

3 3 3 3 3

three

three

three

Thinking Kids®
Carson-Dellosa Publishing LLC
Greensboro, North Carolina

Thinking Kids®
Carson-Dellosa Publishing LLC
PO Box 35665
Greensboro, NC 27425  USA

Printed in the USA • All rights reserved.
01-050181151

ISBN  978-1-4838-4484-8

# 0 1 2 3

# 4 5 6 7

# 8 9 10 11

# 12 13 14 15

# 16 17 18 19

# 20

0

zero

zero zero

zero zero

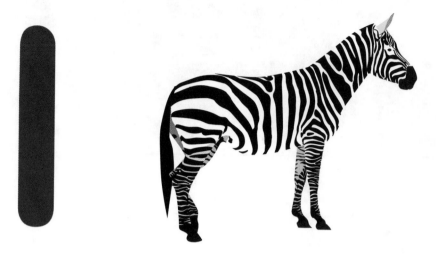

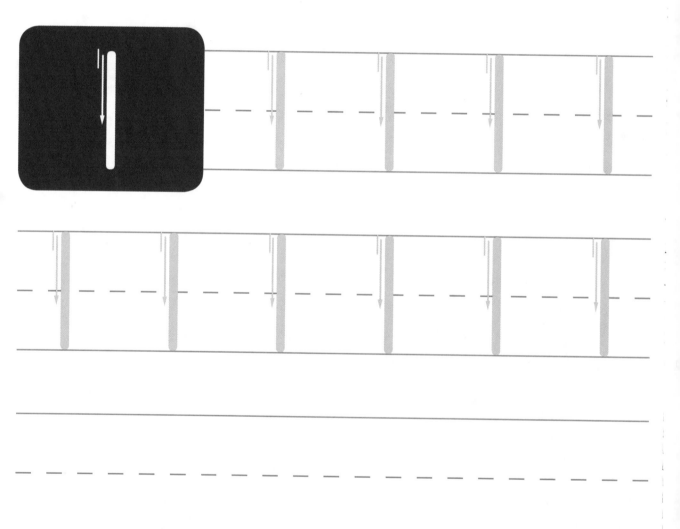

one one

one one

2

2

2 2 2 2

2 2 2 2 2

two two

two two

**3**

3   3   3   3

3   3   3   3   3

three three

three three

four        four

four        four

# 5

5  5  5  5

5  5  5  5  5

five five

five five

# 6

6 6 6

6 6 6 6 6

6 6 6 6 6

six     six

six     six

# 7

seven seven

seven seven

# 8

eight

eight     eight

eight     eight

9

9

nine    nine

nine    nine

# 10

ten          ten

ten          ten

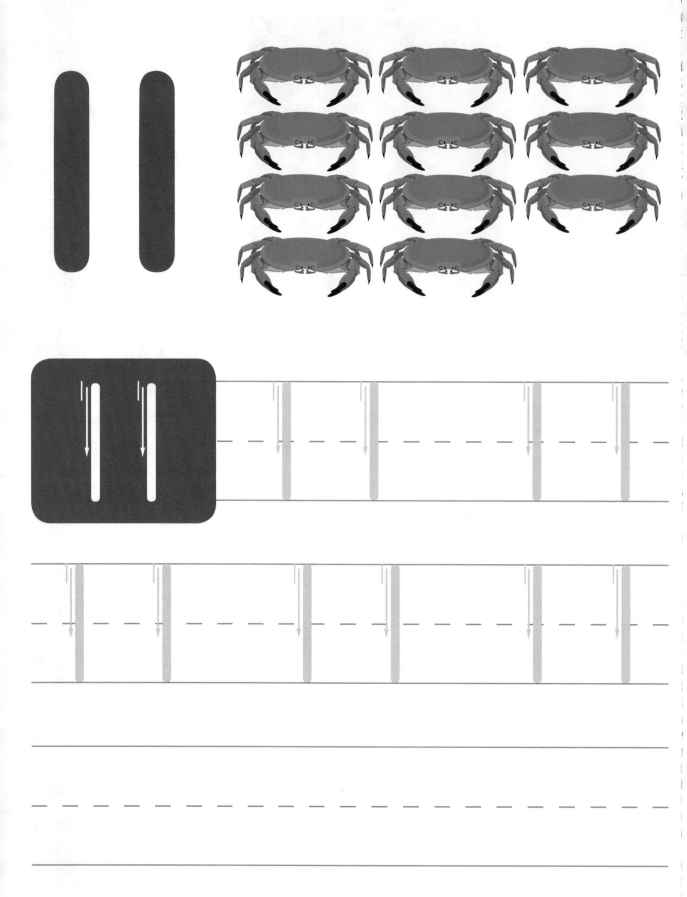

# eleven

eleven

eleven

# 12

12

twelve

twelve

twelve

# 13

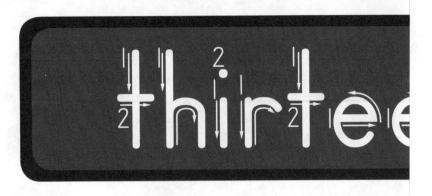

thirteen

thirteen

4

fourteen

fourteen

fourteen

# 15

# fifteen

fifteen

fifteen

# 16

# sixteen

sixteen

sixteen

# 17

# seventeen

seventeen

seventeen

18

# eighteen

eighteen

eighteen

# 19

# nineteen

nineteen

nineteen

# 20

20 20 20

20 20 20

twenty

twenty

twenty

# Count 0 stars.

# Count **I** sun.

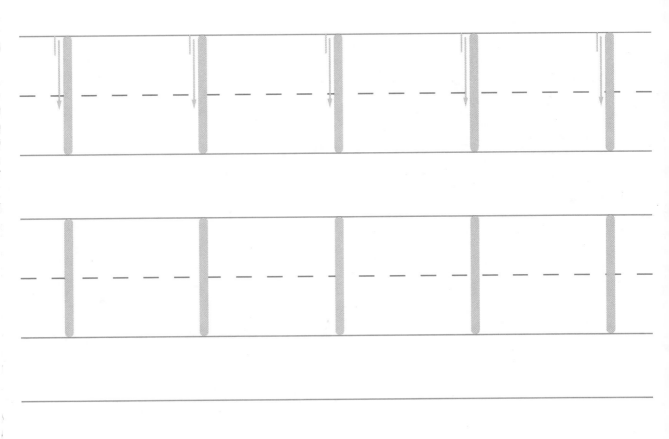

# Count 2 trees.

2 2 2 2 2

2 2 2 2 2

# Count 3 birds.

3 3 3 3 3

3 3 3 3 3

# Count 4 houses.

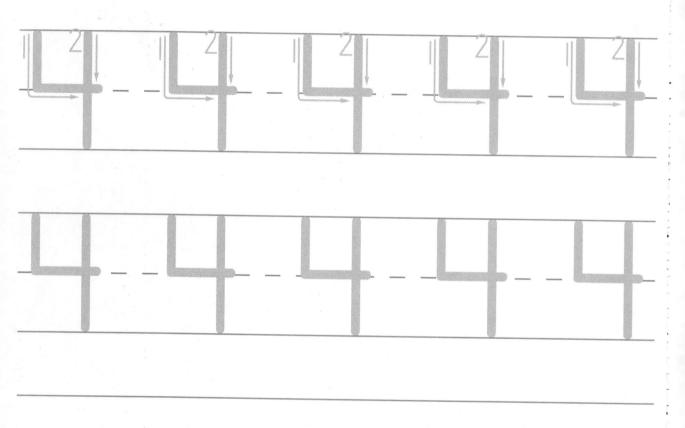

# Count 5 mailboxes.

5 5 5 5 5

5 5 5 5 5

# Count 6 canoes.

6 6 6 6 6

6 6 6 6 6

# Count 7 tents.

7 7 7 7 7

7 7 7 7 7

# Count 8 cans.

8  8  8  8  8

8  8  8  8  8

# Count 9 flowers.

9 9 9 9 9

9 9 9 9 9

# Count 10 balloons.

# Count || flags.

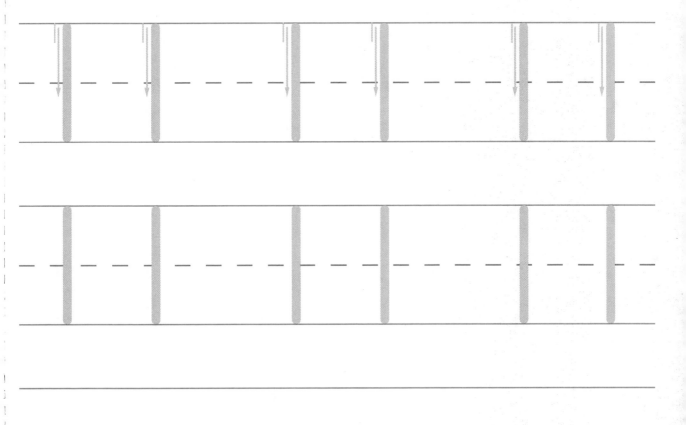

# Count 12 kites.

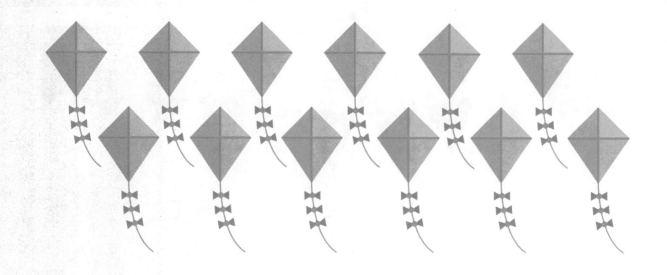

1 2  1 2  1 2

1 2  1 2  1 2

# Count 13 clouds.

1 3  1 3  1 3

1 3  1 3  1 3

# Count 14 carrots.

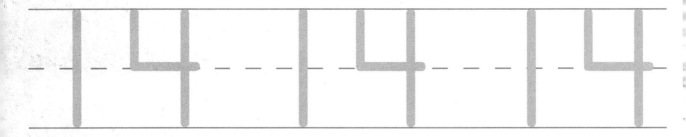

# Count 15 bunnies.

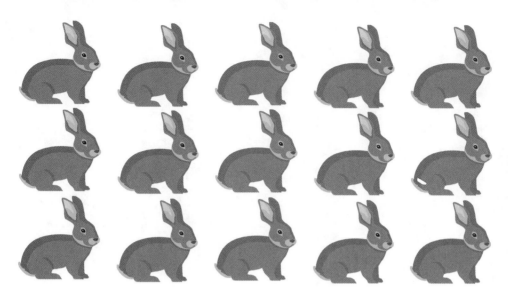

15  15  15

15  15  15

# Count 16 shells.

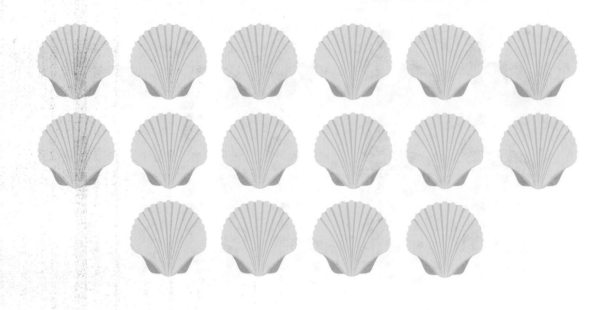

16 16 16

16 16 16

# Count 17 boats.

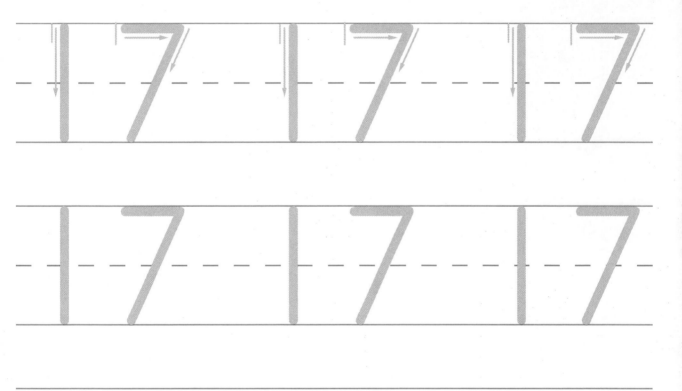

# Count 18 balls.

18 18 18

18 18 18

# Count 19 bats.

# Count 20 leaves.

20 20 20 20

20 20 20

# Count zero toys.

TOYS

zero zero

zero zero

# Count one wagon.

one   one

one   one

# Count two games.

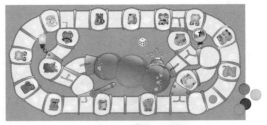

two two

two two

# Count three robots.

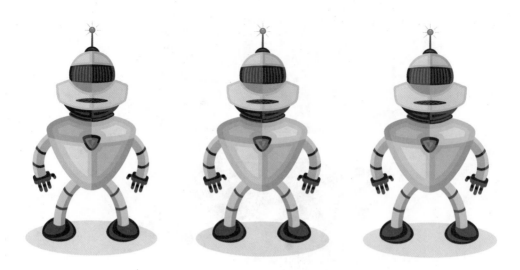

three three

three three

# Count four trains.

four    four

four    four

# Count five bears.

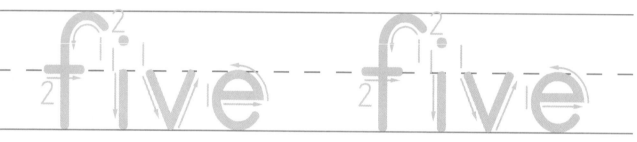

five    five

five    five

# Count six ducks.

six    six

six    six

# Count seven helicopters.

seven seven

seven seven

# Count eight planes.

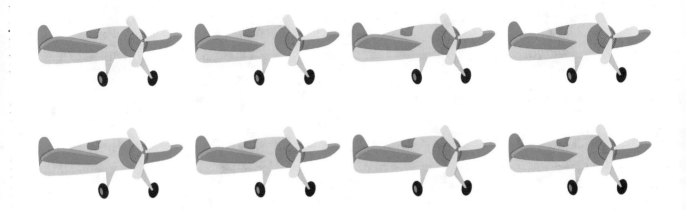

eight eight

eight eight

# Count nine dolls.

nine   nine

nine   nine

# Count ten action figures.

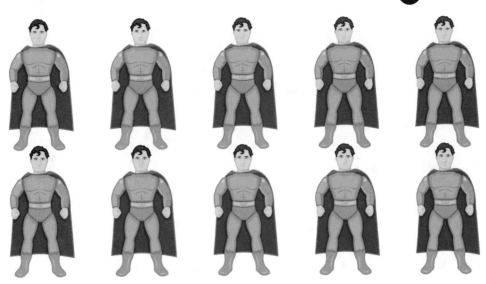

ten    ten

ten    ten

# Count eleven mice.

eleven

eleven

# Count twelve elephants.

twelve

twelve

# Count thirteen trucks.

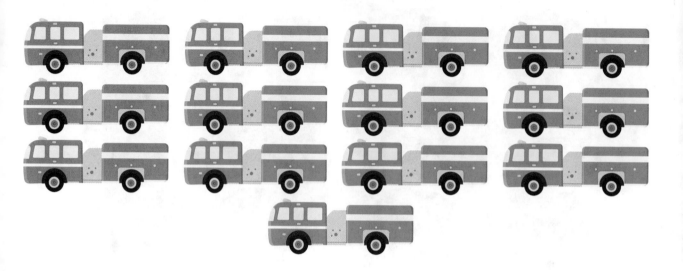

thirteen

# Count fourteen keys.

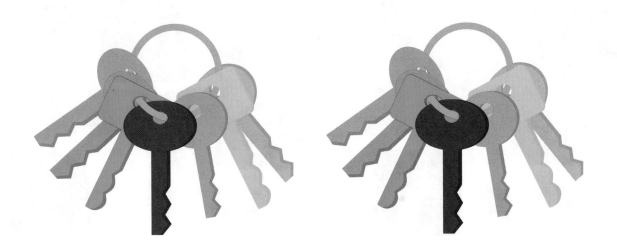

fourteen

fourteen

# Count fifteen blocks.

fifteen

fifteen

# Count sixteen horses.

sixteen

sixteen

# Count seventeen balls.

seventeen

seventeen

# Count eighteen cars.

eighteen

eighteen

# Count nineteen marbles.

nineteen

nineteen

# Count twenty bubbles.

I see ___0___ candles.

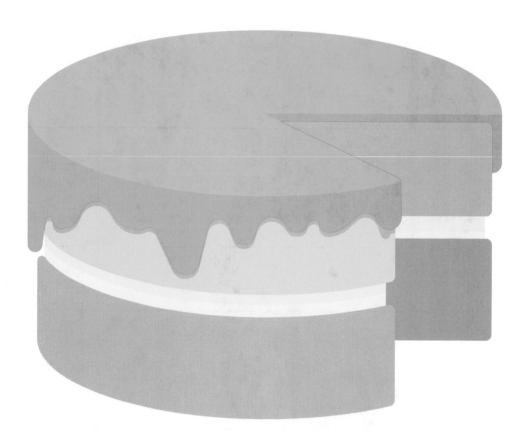

zero

I see _ _ _ 1 _ birthday hat.

one

I see **2** apples.

two

I see _____ 3 _____ bananas.

three

I see ____4____ oranges.

four

I see ___5___ pears.

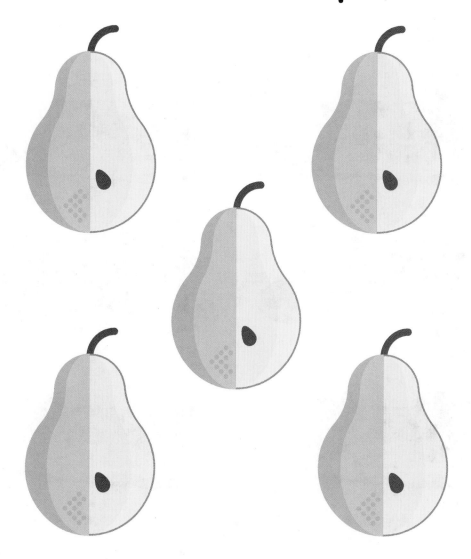

five

I see ___6___ pancakes.

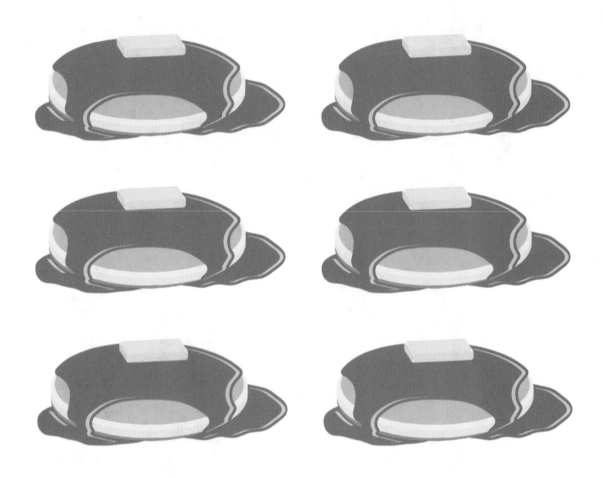

six

I see ___7___ rolls.

seven

I see ___8___ hot dogs.

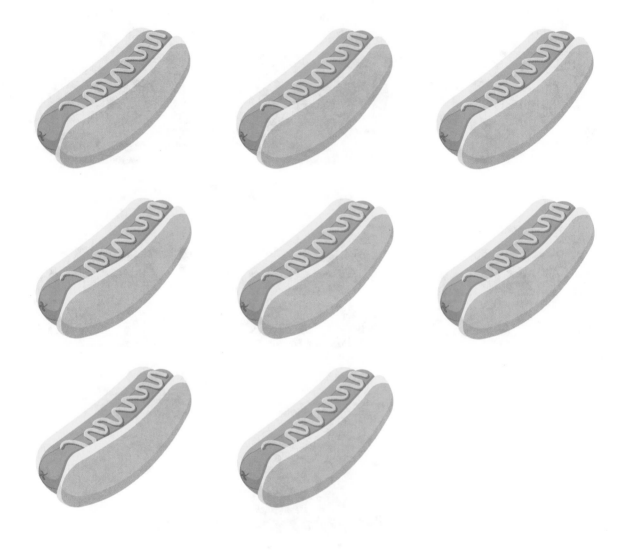

eight

I see ____9____ burgers.

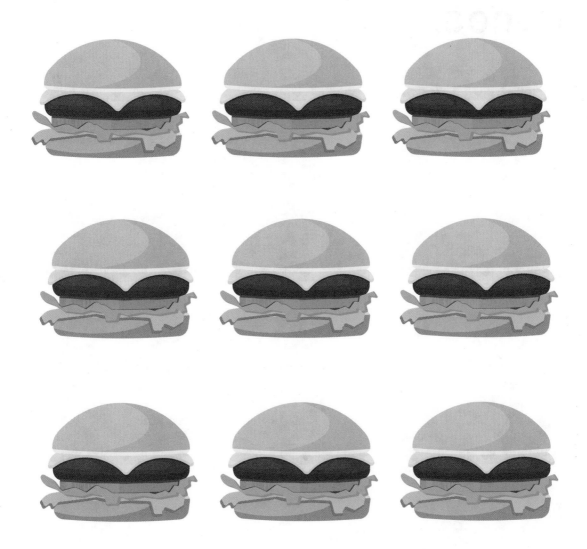

nine

I see __10__ ice-cream cones.

ten

I see _ _ _ 11 _ _ _ cupcakes.

eleven

I see __12__ eggs.

twelve

I see __13__ pans.

thirteen

I see __14__ pumpkins.

fourteen

I see ___15___ tomatoes.

fifteen

I see ___16___ gumballs.

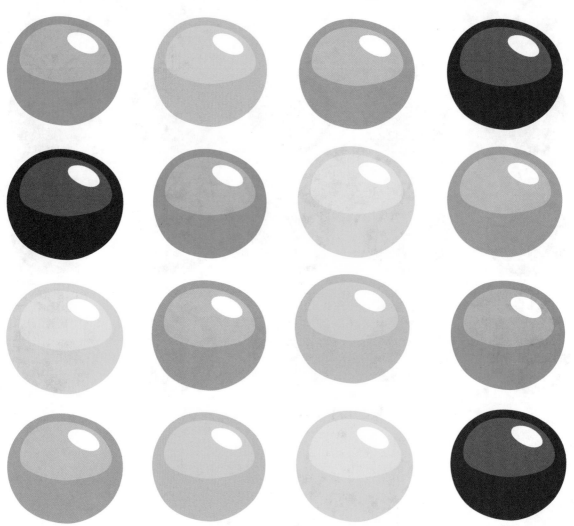

sixteen

I see _____ 17 _____ cookies.

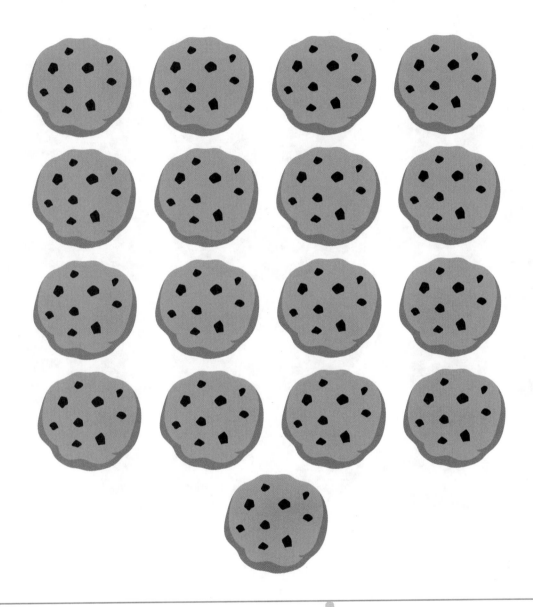

seventeen

I see ___18___ dishes.

eighteen

I see _19_ spoons.

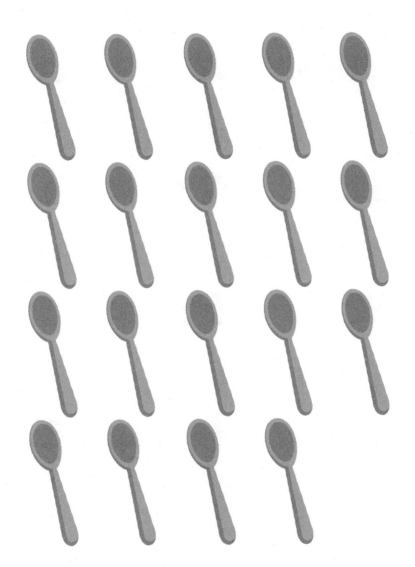

nineteen

I see __20__ umbrellas.

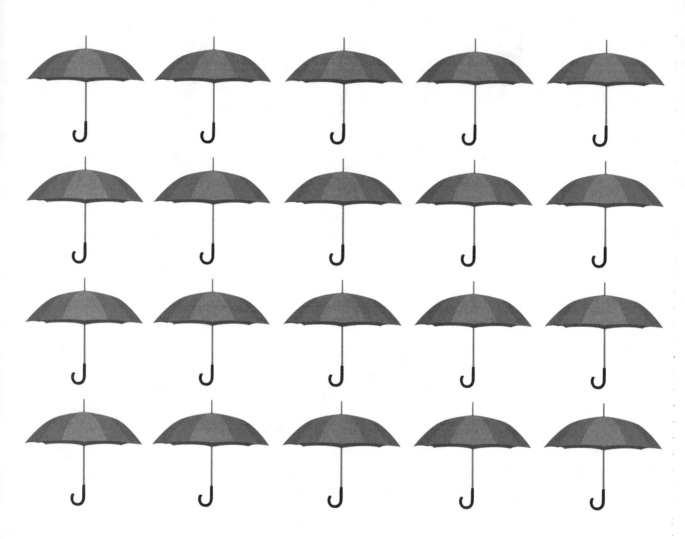

twenty

0 zero

1 one

2 two

3 three

4 four

5 five

6 six

7 seven

8 eight

9   nine

10   ten

11   eleven

12 twelve

13 thirteen

14 fourteen

15 fifteen

16 sixteen

17 seventeen

18 eighteen

19 nineteen

20 twenty

0 1 2 3 4

5 6 7 8 9

10 11 12

13 14 15

16 17 18

19 20

**Directions:** Cut out the flash cards on pages 117-127. Then, have your child use his or her finger to trace the number on each card.

0 1 2 3 4 5

6 7 8 9 10

11 12 13 14 15

16 17 18 19 20

Page is blank for cutting activity on previous page.

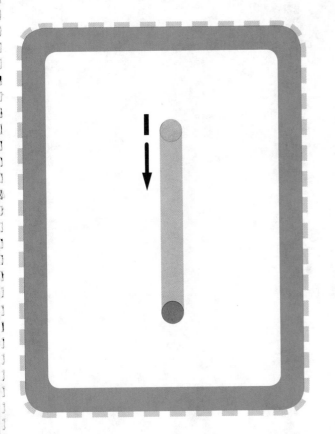

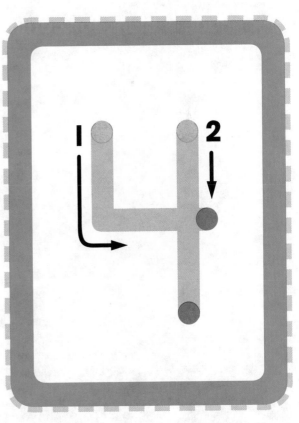

Page is blank for cutting activity on previous page.

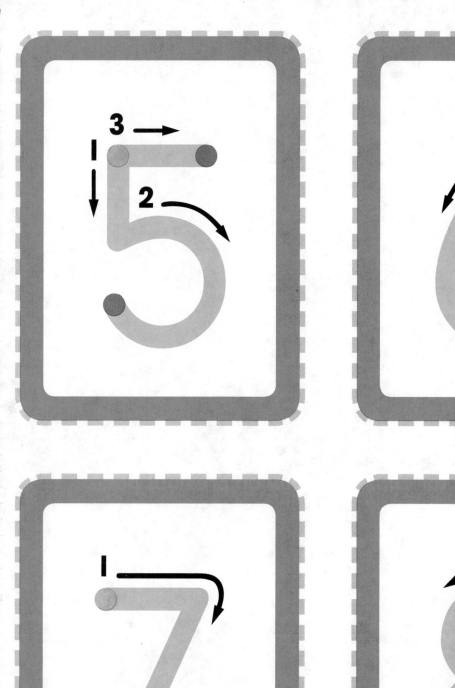

Page is blank for cutting activity on previous page.

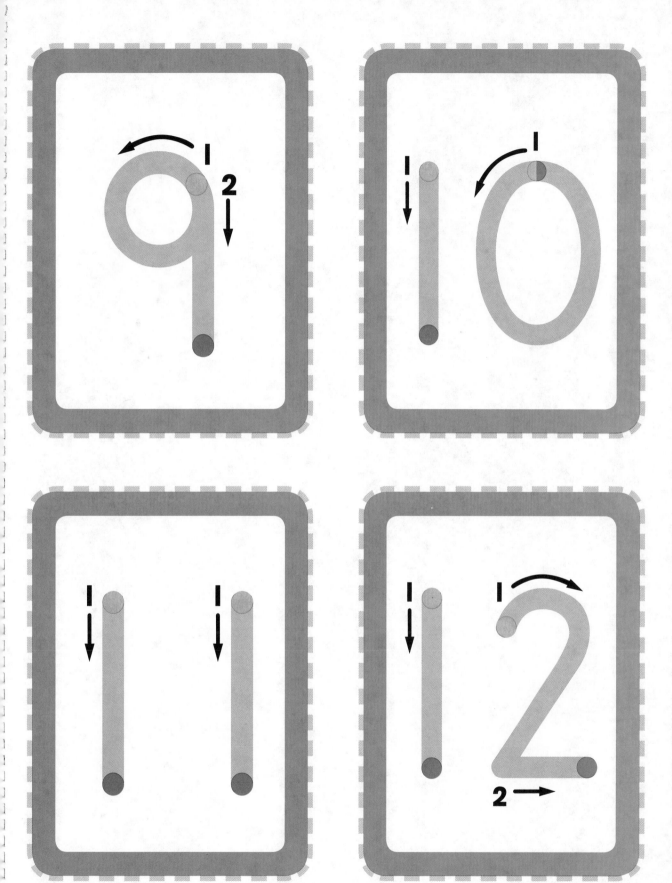

Page is blank for cutting activity on previous page.

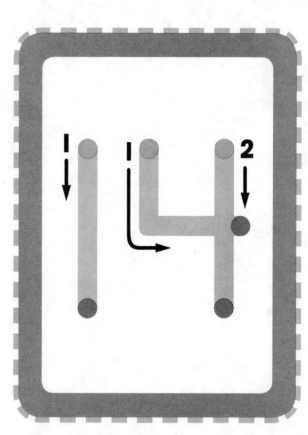

Page is blank for cutting activity on previous page.

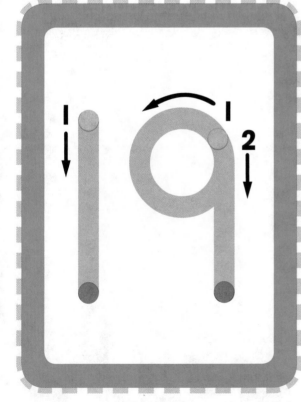
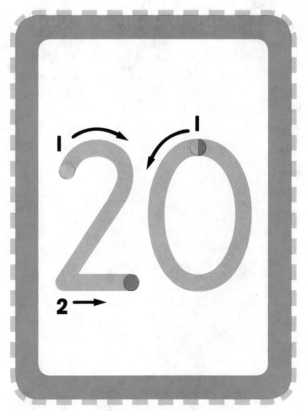

Page is blank for cutting activity on previous page.